Amazon MP3 Store and Cloud Player

Enjoy Music Wherever You Go!

Disclaimer

What Will You Find Here?

Amazon has beaten its competitors by offering an online music player that works really well and offers cloud storage. You can now buy your favorite music tracks from the MP3 store and play them on your Amazon Cloud Player. What's really interesting is the fact that Cloud Player is also integrated with Amazon MP3 app for Android tablets and smartphones.

Why you should visit Amazon's MP3 store daily is something you need to know. If you've been waiting to get the best discount deals on music, there is no reason you should miss out on the deals offered by the MP3 store. This report clearly explains how you can buy MP3's from the store and listen to your favorite music on the Cloud Player.

Of course, you'll know a lot more about live music streaming and downloads, as well as how you can transfer your favorite tracks to the cloud. So, you can have a little more peace of mind with Amazon's latest offering and let us now see how you can interact with the MP3 store and the Cloud Player.

Table of Contents

The Changing Face of Music

Alright, you are a huge fan of the latest technology and you've seen things changing drastically over the last few years. Even music is not the same as it used to be 20 or 30 years back. It has also become digital and you can find lots of exciting gadgets in the market that'll help your play your favorite tracks.

A few gadgets help you take your music everywhere you go. That is you can take your music library to your living room, your favorite restaurant and even to your workplace. But can you access your music tracks if your device gets stolen or add more tracks if your device runs out of storage space?

Most gadgets require you to transfer music via USB, flash drive or any other external storage device. This means your music remains scattered and you have to decide what devices you want to carry along. What's even worse is that after every few days, you have to delete content from the device to make room for new tracks. You can understand this better if you've ever been "out of space".

Moreover, if you want to listen to an older song, you have to literally browse through hundreds of tracks and sometimes, you wouldn't even have the right device with you.

Meet Amazon MP3 Store and Cloud Player

Just imagine if there was a place where you could buy your favorite music tracks and play them on all your devices. There would be no hassle and you would no longer have to sort your gadgets and external device every time you want to listen to your favorite track.

Well, now your life is going to be a lot easier with the help of Amazon Cloud Player. You can check out how it works in more detail as we proceed with the eBook, but here's a brief description for those of you who are really curious.

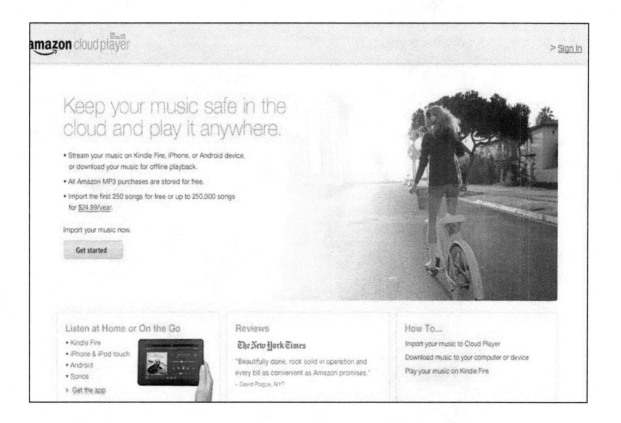

When you buy an MP3 from the Amazon MP3 Store, it is automatically sent to your Amazon Cloud Player. You can say that Amazon Cloud Player is your own online and personal music player. It gives you a chance to download or play your favorite music on any of your devices anytime, anywhere you want. And, you can upload the rest of your tracks to Amazon Cloud Player using the easy to use music importer.

So, your music library is available 24/7 and you can stream live music from any device such as iPad, iPod, Android tablet, smartphone or even your personal computer. Even if you device has limited storage, you still have full access to all the tracks stored on your Cloud Player.

You don't have to worry if you plan to get a new device to play your music. Your music tracks remain secure in the cloud and you can access them right away with the help of Amazon Cloud Player. Remember, with Amazon MP3 store and Cloud Player, your music is with you everywhere you go.

Why You Should Buy Music from Amazon MP3 Store

After reading through the first few pages, you would surely be excited to know more about Amazon MP3 store and Cloud Player. Here's a quick recap about why you should go ahead and browse the amazing offering from Amazon.

You have Access to More than 20 Million Songs

Yes, Amazon MP3 store offers more than 20 million songs that consist of bestselling albums and a vast collection of artists. You can find music albums starting at $7.99 and a single MP3 track would not cost you more than $0.99.

What's really good about this MP3 store is the fact that you can shop for your favorite artists, albums and music tracks from your iPhone, iPod touch, Kindle Fire HD, Android tablet and smartphone. The songs and albums you buy from the Store are directly transferred to Amazon Cloud Player. This means you have a secure backup for your purchase and you can download the track to your device whenever you want.

Shop over **20 million songs** and play your music from the cloud on your **Kindle Fire**, **Android device**, iPad, **iPhone**, **iPod touch**, **Sonos**, Mac or PC with **Amazon Cloud Player**.

100 $5 Albums
On Sale Now

Paradise [Explicit]

Love Songs

Greatest Hits

> See them all

Discover the Best New Music and Deals

Import Your Music Tracks to Amazon Cloud Player

Amazon Cloud Player serves as a secure backup for your MP3 tracks and you can access your files anytime, anywhere. You can also take advantage of the easy to use "music importer" to make your own music tracks instantly available in Cloud Player. Remember, the first 250 songs you buy from the Amazon MP3 store are transferred to

Cloud Player for free and you can import up to 250,000 songs by paying just $24.99 per year.

Your Music is Everywhere You Go

You can easily play and download music from Amazon Cloud Player to your Kindle Fire, iPad, iPhone, iPod touch, Android tablets and smartphones. Moreover, you can download all your tracks to play them even if you are not connected to the internet.

Shop for music in the app and play it anywhere, with the same low prices and great selection you can find on the Amazon MP3 website. Or import your own music library to the cloud, then stream or download your MP3s to your Android phone or tablet, so you can listen to your music collection anywhere. Get the app from the Amazon Appstore, or get the app from Google Play.

Technical Details

· App requires Android OS 2.1 and up
· PDF and video content is currently not available for purchase on the Amazon MP3 Android app

Want to Buy Amazon MP3?

If you want to buy an MP3 from Amazon MP3 store, you must first log in to your valid Amazon account. In addition, you also need to set up your 1-Click payment method and provide a valid U.S billing address.

In case you don't have an Amazon account, you can create one by visiting Amazon.com. Make sure you follow the instructions that appear on the screen. Once you have created your Amazon account, you can visit the Amazon MP3 store to search and shop for your favorite tracks.

You can access the Amazon MP3 store from your web browser, Android tablet, smartphone and Kindle tablets. If there's anything you want to buy, simply click or tap the title to go to the details page.

Tap or click **"Buy MP3 album with 1-Click"** or **"Buy MP3 song with 1-Click"** to purchase your desired item. As mentioned earlier, your MP3 will directly be moved to the Amazon Cloud Player.

Buying Amazon MP3 on iPhone or iPod

You can now browse and shop for your favorite music albums using the new Amazon Cloud Player app for iOS. This app gives you a chance to explore music collections in the Amazon MP3 Store and you can play your "purchase" on your Apple devices including iPad, iPhone or iPod touch.

One thing you need to remember is that only U.S. customers can buy music from Amazon MP3 Store using the app for iPhone and iPod touch. If you want to buy an MP3, open the Safari browser on your Apple device (iPhone or iPod touch) and go to the Amazon MP3 store.

Search for items you want to buy and confirm your purchase by tapping **Buy**. Your item will be charged using your 1 Click Payment Method and the album or track will be transferred to the Amazon Cloud Player.

Give Amazon MP3 as a Gift

Amazon MP3 store also allows you to give most Amazon MP3s as a gift to your family and friends. The person receiving the gift can either play or download the track from Amazon Cloud Player or exchange the MP3 for an Amazon.com Gift Card.

If you want to buy a track for a friend or family member, first log in to your Amazon.com account and visit the Amazon MP3 store. Browse for the track you want to give as a gift and then click **Give as a Gift** that appears under the **Buy** button.

The track or album you buy will be sent to the e-mail address you specify shortly after you confirm the order.

You will be happy to know that Amazon MP3 given as gifts can be downloaded easily to your computer and you can also play the track directly in Amazon Cloud Player using a compatible device.

If you want to download the song you have received as a gift, open the email message and then click **Get your gift now**. You will then be guided to your gift on Amazon.com.

All you have to do next is click **Download your MP3 gift** and enter your Amazon.com account details if prompted.

You will see a confirmation page where you can click **Download to your computer** to save the track on your computer's hard disk. It is better if you download and install the Amazon MP3 Downloader on your computer if you don't have it already.

If you don't want to download your gift, you can click **Play your music in Cloud Player** and play your MP3 track in Amazon Cloud Player.

Download Music to Your Computer

Using Amazon MP3 Downloader

The **Amazon MP3 Downloader** can be used on Windows or Macintosh PCs and you can use it along with your web browser to make your download experience more interesting.

Presently, the Amazon MP3 downloader is compatible with Windows XP, Windows 7 and Windows Vista. If you are using a Mac computer, you should be running Mac OS X 10.4 on Intel-based hardware. For Mac, you also need to have Adobe AIR version 3.3.x.

If you are interested to know how Amazon MP3 downloader can help you, you need to read this. Well, this exciting software helps you download music tracks from Amazon Cloud Player and send it to iTunes or Windows Media Player. To install the Amazon MP3 Downloader, first log in to your Amazon.com account and then go to http://www.amazon.com/gp/dmusic/help/amd.html/.

Install the Amazon MP3 Downloader

We recommend installing the Amazon MP3 Downloader before your first purchase. It is required for multiple-song downloads and makes downloading songs fast and easy.

Click **Install** to install the Amazon MP3 Downloader and save all eligible past and future Amazon music purchases and matched music to Cloud Player.

☐ I have read and accept the Terms of Use.

Install   For Windows XP, Windows Vista, and Windows 7. Download takes less than 90 seconds.

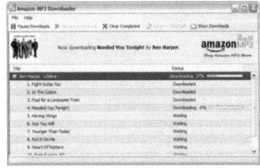

Click **Install** and follow the detailed instructions mentioned on the Amazon MP3 Downloader page to start using the software. There is no need to specify your operating system as it will be detected automatically.

Downloading Tracks to Your Computer

Once you download and install the Amazon MP3 Downloader on your computer, you can easily import your Amazon MP3 tracks and albums from Amazon Cloud Player. To save the tracks to your computer, log in to your Amazon Cloud Player account and mark the check boxes next to MP3 tracks and albums you want to download.

Click **Download** and your music will automatically be added to your Windows Media Player, iTunes or desktop.

Note: You may be prompted to install the Amazon MP3 Downloader in case you haven't installed it yet. However, if you want to download a single song, you can do it easily using your browser and choose **Skip installation** when prompted to install the Amazon MP3 Downloader.

How You Can Find Your Download on the Computer

Music or MP3 tracks you download from Amazon Cloud Player are automatically saved in your Amazon Cloud Player app on the device. You can find the tracks in your default download folder on your computer running Windows or Macintosh computer.

If you cannot find your favorite MP3 tracks on your computer, first launch the Amazon MP3 Downloader on your computer and then click **View Download Folder**. To make things easier for you, Amazon Mp3 downloader saves your music within the "My Music" folder on your computer running Windows. You can find the tracks in the "Music" folder if you are using a Mac computer.

If you want to change the default download folder for the Amazon MP3 Downloader, you can do it easily by changing the settings. Here's how you can do it. Go to the Amazon MP3 Downloader and then click File > Preferences.

Music Tracks and AMZ Files

You can see a dialog box asking you to open or save an *.amz* file whenever you buy an MP3 (from the Amazon MP3 store), using your computer's web browser. This message normally appears if you have the Amazon MP3 Downloader installed on your computer, but there's nothing to worry about.

If you make a purchase on your computer, select **Open**, not **Save** if prompted. Opening AMZ files launches the Amazon MP3 Downloader and your track will automatically be downloaded to your computer.

Know How You Can Import Music to the Cloud

Now, you can add your favorite music tracks from your computer, iTunes or Windows Media Player to Amazon Cloud Player. And, all this is possible using the **Amazon Music Importer** for Cloud Player. You can easily transfer your tracks to the cloud using this importer but you need to have Adobe Flash installed and enabled on your computer to use this software.

If you want to install the Amazon Music Importer, first go to Amazon Cloud Player for Web using your web browser. You can use any popular browser such as Firefox, Internet Explorer or Safari.

Click **Import Your Music** and then click **Download Now**. Your installation should start within a few seconds and make sure you follow the instructions that appear on your screen.

Adding Songs to the Amazon Cloud Player

Once successfully installed on your computer, Amazon Music Importer will ask for permission to automatically search your Music libraries. You can also choose to scan the folders manually, however this may take more time.

Your music tracks in iTunes, Windows Media Player and other folders will appear in the Amazon Music Importer and you can click **Import all** to send all your tracks to the cloud. Click **Import selected** if you want to transfer selected tracks to the cloud.

Remember, you can import up to 250 MP3 tracks to Cloud Player for free and moving up to 250,000 songs will only cost $24.99. MP3 tracks you buy from Amazon MP3 are automatically transferred to Amazon Cloud Player and do not count towards the basic limit of 250 tracks.

File Formats Supported on the Cloud Player

Amazon Cloud Player can only play music and tracks having the following file formats.

1. mp3

2. m4a and AAC files for Windows and Mac including purchases from iTunes store.

3. wma (Windows Media Audio files)

4. wav

5. aiff (Audio Interchange Audio Format)

6. flac (Free Lossless Audio Codec files)

7. ogg (Ogg Vorbis audio files)

Streaming Music from the Cloud

You can listen to your favorite music in Amazon Cloud Player using Cloud Player for Web, Amazon Cloud Player app or Amazon MP3 app. Your music can be streamed on your computer or any other compatible device.

To stream your music, go to Amazon Cloud Player on your computer or mobile device. Select a track and then click **Play.** Your music should immediately start playing if you are connected to the internet. If your music is taking lots of time to load, check your wireless signals and try moving closer to your wireless access point.

Your music can take time to play if someone else in your home is using the same internet connection. Music and videos typically require more time to stream if your internet connection is used to playing games, or watching online videos. Make sure you have the best internet connection to enjoy uninterrupted music.

Create and Edit a Playlist in the Cloud Player

If you want to create a playlist in Amazon Cloud Player, simply mark the check boxes next to tracks you want to add to your new playlist. Click **Add to playlist** once you are done. Similarly, you can also delete music files from Amazon Cloud Player. Here's how you can do it. Mark the boxes next to the music tracks you want to delete and then click "Delete" to remove the items from your Cloud Player list. If you want to permanently remove these music files from the cloud, click **Deleted Items** from the menu and then click **Empty all deleted items**.

Buying and Listening to Music on Kindle Devices

Kindle Fire HD 8.9" and 7"

You can search and shop for music in the Amazon MP3 store using Kindle Fire HD 8.9" and 7". All you have to do is tap **Music** from your Home Screen and then tap **Store**. You will be guided to the Amazon MP3 store where you can find the best MP3 deals and promotions. If you cannot find your favorite track, you can always browse for music using the different categories such as New Releases, Bestsellers, and Genres.

Buying Music from Amazon MP3 Store

To simplify your search further, tap the search bar at the top and enter your term. Tap the magnifying glass next to the search box to see the results. Once you've found the MP3 track or album you would like to buy, simply tap **Buy** or **Get**. Your order will then be processed using your 1-Click payment method and your music will automatically be sent to Amazon Cloud Player.

You can tap **Go to your library** to listen to the song you've just purchased and even download it to your Kindle device. If you want to browse for more tracks, tap **Continue shopping** to return to the Amazon MP3 Store.

Playing Music with Amazon Cloud Player

You can tap **Music** from your Kindle Fire HD Home Screen and then tap Cloud to view the items present in your Cloud Library. The "Cloud" library features all music you've purchased from the Amazon MP3 store and you can explore your collection by playlists, artists, albums or songs.

Note:

Music in Cloud Library can only be played when your Kindle Fire HD is connected to the internet. You have to download the tracks to your device if you want to play them without a Wi-Fi or WAN connection. (WAN connection presently is only available for Kindle Fire HD 8.9" Model.)

If you want to import your music files from Kindle Fire HD 8.9" or 7" to Amazon Cloud Player, you can do it easily using the Amazon Music Importer.

This eBook should answer all your questions related to the Amazon MP3 store and Cloud Player. Once you start using Amazon Cloud Player, you would never worry about having access to your music files wherever you go. Don't forget to download the Cloud Player app for your Kindle Fire HD, iPad, iPod touch or Android devices to stay connected with your music. With Amazon MP3 store and Cloud Player, you can easily say that there is no limitation to buying and listening to your favorite songs and albums.